LAMBS TO THE SLAUGHTER

*Love, Scams and true stories
of Thai girls and more*

By Dave James

Copyright © 2019 Dave James

CONTENTS

INTRODUCTION

Everything you read here are true accounts of actual situations or things I have personally been through and stories about people or events that have happened in the crazy land of smiles – Amazing Thailand.

OK, let's start with who I am and what has happened to me over the years. You can call me Dave, I'm semi-retired, own a resort hotel with my wife and currently live here in Thailand. I'm going to be a little cautious and change the names of people I write about as many of them are regular guests at our hotel and I don't want to cause them or us any issues.

I've been coming to Thailand for the last 27 years, the first time was a holiday with a mate in 1991. I fell in love as most guys do and that's where my life changed from boring to incredibly exciting and exotic. I've been married 4 times, and had several long term relationships in between. Currently still living with my wonderful Thai wife and very happily married for over 10 years, but it wasn't always like this… As you will see later in all my stories and accounts.

Two sayings that I remember and stick in my mind

"If you're on your way to heaven and your plane stops at Thailand – GET OFF"

This was on an adult travel brochure and was the main incentive for me to come and see what it really meant… and I agree totally…. It can be the most fun place on earth or a complete nightmare as you will read later…

> *"You can take a girl out of the bar BUT you can
> never take the bar out of the girl"*

This little saying is also, so very true and EVERYONE I meet has told me,

> *"Their wife or girlfriend is different."*

Well I can tell you this for starters, after 27 years experience of Thailand - That's absolute rubbish … I would say about 95% of all Thai women have only one ultimate goal… In fact, it must be taught in the Thai schools, as even the nicer girls and older women that have NEVER even worked in the entertainment industry, bars, massage etc. have this mentality.

They all think, the answer to their problems is to "marry a foreigner" (Farang) because ALL Farangs are rich and will build them a house and buy them gold and support their families for the rest of their lives.

To them, it's like winning the lottery, until that is, they get to the UK or wherever and realise that their dream, is nothing like they had thought or been led to believe. They soon learn, it's far more expensive to live in other countries… Unless of course, they really did get lucky and found a stupid cash cow that has more money than sense. And as you will see in my stories, there are hundreds of stupid cash cows and they never learn…

I'm going to start in the first few chapters with a few different stories and events of all the interesting and incredibly stupid things Farangs and the girls do. Then I will add a few of my own and believe me, they are… well… let me put it this way, I feel like I have had ten lives… not one.

CHAPTER 1

Paul from Canada

I now have Paul's permission to publish his full story and he even suggested, I write a book with all my stories! So here's his story... the first part was written within a week it happening but since then several new twists and turns have happened.

Paul arrived a few days ago in a terrible state and very upset and scared to say the least, as two Thai girls brought him to our hotel as a sort of "safe house" because they saw him wandering around in a local village not far from us with his two large suit cases after being kicked out of his girlfriend's house by the police. It turned out that one of the policeman, was his girlfriend's boyfriend. She loved to gamble and it seems that poor Paul refused to keep funding her and was duly kicked out by the girl, the policeman and her family.

The two girls who brought him to our hotel wanted to help him and they even brought him food and snacks a couple of times a day. I only just met him personally yesterday as he had been hiding in his room for 3 days, scared to go out in case the police and his crazy ex girlfriend found him before he flies home to Canada in a few days' time.

I heard, he had been sending her money, approx. 50,000 Baht (over GBP £1000) per month! I kid you not 50,000... For about a year or more... Yet, the average wage in Thailand is only 15 – 20,000 Baht per month. Truly mental....

My wife had been chatting to the two girls who have been explaining what happened.

Today I hear, the girlfriend and the policeman have been looking for him and had asked the 2 girls where they had taken him... They told her (and the Thai policeman boyfriend) that he was at our hotel and we had already informed the Thai Immigration office that he is staying at our hotel. (A requirement here for all hotels with foreign guests) This has apparently scared the policeman and her away because the Immigration police have a lot more power than the normal police.

The reason they were looking for poor Paul was to try to extract even more money out of him as he was their major source of income for the last couple of years. Paul is now out of his room and feeling a lot more protected now the immigration office are aware of him and he's been chatting to my wife, myself and the other guests and is swimming in the pool and in a much better mood now.

You may be thinking he may have been saved BUT.....

Paul has now started to make plans to come back in about 6 months' time and start a new relationship with one of the 2 girls that had rescued him! However, the story with her is, that she is "still married to a Thai guy" but all is not well in their relationship. The girl has told her friend that she needs to get rid of her Thai husband before she can start a full on relationship with her new cash cow – Paul.

Now I'm sure she is "truly in love with him" and it has absolutely nothing to do with the 50,000 Baht PER MONTH he was sending to the last girl!

UPDATE 6 am on 24th March

We helped Paul escape yesterday evening at 5 PM. He was supposed to checkout this morning at 7 AM and fly back to Bangkok and then home to Canada. Two of the vampires (girls) were here at 5 AM knocking on his bungalow window, so my wife had to go down and tell them he had left yesterday. They only left after an hour or so of talking to my wife!

So what happened yesterday? Well Paul was still unaware, that the girl he was supposed to be going out with now, was still married and she was playing him along with her friend to set him up for supporting her (sending money) when he got home with the promise they will be together on his return to Thailand in September.

My wife told me that these two girls were really bad girls and well known in the area, so I decided to go tell Paul the truth, to try to help him understand what was going on.... I told him the girl who he was (quickly becoming besotted with) was still married and not even separated like he had been told. I also told him that she had been called by the first girlfriend's policeman boyfriend and asked, where he was?

She told the policeman, that he was at our hotel and the emigration knows where he is. This frightened the policeman (as the Immigration police have much more power).

So Paul was very shocked at my revelation and clearly upset, but thanked me for helping him see through all their bullshit. So I asked him what exactly happened with the first girl he left and supported for a year.

He told me,

"I was only there for a few days and she kept wanting money to buy things and then the straw that broke the camel's back was, she asked me to buy her a cow (20,000 Baht)! I told her no way, and she got all abusive and stormed out of the house. She returned at 11 PM drunk, with her policeman boyfriend!!! And they both kicked me out. I was then taken in by her friend and her husband (also a policeman), and for the next week they made me buy them and another 3 people meals 3 x a day, beer every day and then the policeman was trying to get me to give him more money! I got mad and left their house and that's when

the other two girls found me wandering down the road with my cases and brought me to your hotel."

Then Paul told me, that the day before, the girl turned up with another "friend" who explained that the first girlfriend, was a bad lady and that she was playing a game with him to extract money. This new "friend" then went on to call "one of her rich boyfriends in the USA" and show him how easy it was to get money out of foreign men. She also has an American husband but he only comes for 3 months per year (so she has a few other boyfriends on the go as well)

Paul and I have no idea why she wanted to do this in front of him, I can only imagine it was to show off in front of her friend or him or whatever!

Paul then said, "She called up this guy and was all sexy and sweet on the phone and doing a video call showing herself by our swimming pool and saying how she wants to get a similar pool at her house. He agrees to buy her a pool and then a bit more loving chat and the call ended. She turned to him and said "SEE that is how easy it is, he will buy me a swimming pool now because he is a racing car driver and very rich."

I told Paul,

"But you do realise that your "new" girlfriend is learning all this shit about how to get money out of unsuspecting foreigners from her friend...!"

He looked at me all stony faced and said,

"Yes I can see what's going on now, but she is coming here later and we are going to the shopping centre and see a movie."

I then told him,

"Well, I suggest you just play along, as you're leaving in the morning and you don't need any issues today or this evening, just pretend you have not heard anything I have told you."

In the afternoon he arrived back and there are now 4 girls with him... all carrying bags of shopping and a kilo of prawns each... He had been treating them all again…!

My wife calls me and tells me he has cancelled the 7 AM taxi for the morning and the girls are taking him to the airport. Not good… she tells me because her husband knows she is seeing him now.

She then told me what one of the other girls had told her.

About 10 minutes later, the girls all leave and Paul is sitting by the pool. So I walk over and ask him,

"Do you want to swap stories because I have heard some more details?"

"Yes OK" he says. Then starts telling me about how there was a misunderstanding and she really is in love with him and how they are really separated and her husband is gone etc.

"That's not what I've heard mate."

His face looked worried again.

"I heard you have cancelled the taxi for the morning! I think you need to know some facts before you jump in a car with these girls in the morning. YOU DO want to catch your flight I assume? Yesterday her husband followed you and his wife to the shopping centre and saw you together. On her return home ALL her windows were smashed in her house and she had a massive fight with her husband."

I also told him that, the new girlfriend, was planing to get him to help her get a passport and a visa for Canada and when there. And if Paul did not give her money, she could find someone else and would send money back to her "husband to clear his debts". (This was obviously a ploy to get the husband to agree to a divorce so she could capture Paul.)

Paul was stunned again to say the least, clearly upset because he has had his feelings shattered once again. He was very quiet for a while and then said,

"I need to get out of here now! Can you call me a taxi and I will go to a hotel in Khon Kaen and in the morning go straight to the airport."

I told him that was a great plan but, do not tell them anything (which hotel or your plans) until you are on the plane, as they could quite easily try to be at the airport and cause a scene and demand money etc.

He agreed and then 2 of the 4 girls he went out with that day showed upon a motorbike.... They had come to warn him about the girl he was seeing but they could not get him to understand them before, as they couldn't speak any English. They told my wife they felt so sorry for him and everything he had been through, and wanted to help him. They were actually very genuine and clearly upset, and one older girl was actually crying as she told us, she tried to tell him several times, but he didn't understand her.

This at least restored my own faith in humanity as obviously not all Thai girls are as cruel and calculating as some of the ones I am writing about here.

The taxi arrived and Paul left to an unknown hotel in Khon Kaen.... Not even we knew which hotel he escaped to.

In the morning at 5 AM, the new "money sucker girlfriend" was at our hotel with her friend looking for him, and my wife informed me that, she had been calling him all evening but he was not answering her calls or text messages, that's why she came to the hotel early to find out why. My wife just informed them that he took a taxi yesterday at 5 PM and he told us, he was visiting a friend.

Update 25th March

Paul did make it to the airport and we heard later that the girl and her friend had actually gone to the airport to try to find him but they came home unsuccessful as he must have checked in and gone directly through the departure gate.

Update 1st November

Paul came back to Thailand and brought his new girlfriend with him... to introduce her to us. A very nice lady, it seems... but we have since found out that she is a school teacher in a town not too far from here. She is heavily in debt (owes millions of Baht) and is leaving her school teaching position to start a shop... She is about 48 years of age (Paul is 52) and she was only 5 years away from claiming her government pension! Not only that, government workers and school teachers, not only get a pension after 25 years of service, they also get **FREE hospital and dental treatment for themselves and their husband for life**.

The question is.... Why is she throwing that all away?

Obviously, Paul is funding everything, including the shop idea (Lease, stock etc.) and I don't know if he is aware of her debts and reason for her to walk away from her teaching job. My wife says it's probably because her debts are so great, they already deduct loan payments from her salary every month, and will continue even with her pension... so she feels it's better to start a new life with Paul.

Update 15th November,

My wife told me... They got married last week! I wonder why we didn't get an invite to the wedding... Must have been a very small private wedding. Oh dear, things are running a bit fast now and he is applying for a visa to take her back to Canada... That's going to be very expensive... And what about the shop! That will be run by a family member... until they realise there are too many shops already struggling and selling the same plastic goods she intends to sell.... And all the money and stock is gone... But make no mistake, they will milk him for money until.

So how did Paul meet this new lady? .... On the internet... He fell in love with the first lady that told him... she loved him and wanted to go live with him in Canada... Before he had even come here and met her in real life –

You cannot make this shit up...!

I give up on Paul now, he is totally blind and cannot see what's happening for the life of him... He's a great guy but is head over heels in love with this woman... and she... has just won the lottery.

Update 1st February

Honestly, you can't make this stuff up... we have now heard that Paul's new wife is looking for another man on the internet.... Apparently, he can't get her a visa because he does not have enough money in the bank and does not own his own property and has told her she has to wait about a year because they also need a police report and it takes 1 year... That cannot be true as I believe a police report usually only takes a week.

As far as I'm aware, Paul knows nothing about his new wife's activities. So what's really happened is, she has found out Paul is not as rich as she thought and because she has already left her job and is basically in hiding from her debtors... and Paul cannot get her the visa she desperately wanted.... She is looking for a new cash cow.

CHAPTER 2

James from the USA

H ere is another guy (James from the USA) that has stayed at our resort several times in the past but this last time, he was alone and had booked a whole month.

James turned up and was distraught to say the least, he had moved all his stuff out and was storing it at a Thai friend's house. He had been kicked out of his house after 14 years of living together but he loved his dogs and cats and even his "crazy" wife.

He claimed she was an alcoholic and wouldn't listen to reason, she would go out with her friends and come back drunk and abusive. Everyone had advised him, to get out of the relationship for years but as he travelled back and forth to the USA over the last 14 years, he just kept going back to her and his house I suppose, supporting her and the whole family, kids, dogs, cars and everything for 14 years.

The problem is, he built the house himself over the years and feels that he is losing everything. But the reality in Thailand is... You cannot own land and it is extremely rare for any "Farang" to come out of any relationship with any money, house or land.

She even had a child with another foreign guy who also sends her money and turns up periodically to visit his daughter and her. It is also claimed, by other villagers, that she has a Thai boyfriend living with her as well, whenever James and the other boyfriend were not around...!

Now, I like James a lot and we hit it off really well as friends and we've had many a beer and chat together by the pool but he will not accept that his wife / girlfriend had another "two guys" shagging her. He assured me... that she only had "him" as a sleeping partner and all the rumours were all totally untrue!

So what can we do when someone will not accept the truth... Even when it slaps them in the face! Then we heard, he had moved back in with her and had paid all the outstanding bills again, (car payments, dog and cat food, electric, cable TV and the rest) and said he was only going to support her to the tune of 15,000 – 20,000 Baht per month from now on!!!

Even if she had a proper job in the bank or something, she could not earn that!

He was living here in Thailand full time on a retirement visa but as the relationship is so stormy, he now says he's going to live between the USA and Thailand like before he retired and still support her!

It wasn't long before she kicked him out again.... A few weeks and then he went back to the USA. I think her issue is that James can be a bit intense... No I will rephrase that, he is very intense. He's a real moaner and actually complains about "everything." Although, I really like him as a friend, I can only take him in small doses as the conversation is always very one sided and he actually believes all the rubbish going on in his head about the situation of his alcoholic wife and family etc. He needs to cut the strings and stay away from her and find someone new... There are so many to choose from... It's so sad to watch him cling on and throw more and more money at this woman who clearly is not interested in him... Just the money.

Update 3rd Nov

James is back and he phoned me for a chat and he is back in Thailand trying to get back with her...! but she's having none of it... She's now told him, her parents are both alcoholics and have moved in and trashed the house... He then told me, he has just received a tax rebate, that he had been fighting for, because he was supporting his wife here in Thailand for the last 10 years or so... He received about a million baht (US$30,000). And he only went and told her...!

Surprise... surprise... Now she's interested in him again.... Oh My God.... you cannot make this shit up... But get this, she still won't let him move back in... So he's gone to live up north in Chiang Mai for a month while he keeps talking with her on the phone. He says he feels he has to help her with her bills and the dogs and the car and is sending her money again.... He is truly out of his mind and will not listen to reason.

Update January 2019

James has called me and asked if he can pop in for a chat.... He said he's moved back in with her and all is OK.... We had a good chat... no I'll rephrase that, I listened to him for an hour as he doesn't listen to anything I say, so I was pretty quiet and then he left... telling me he had lots of stuff to sort out, fix up the fence and clean up the house... Not a week later and he is back telling me he has booked a flight and is off Chiang Mai again as it's not working out... I told him there are 10,000's of nice girls out there and he is retired and has a fantastic $2000 per month pension so WHY oh WHY is he still clinging on to this crazy woman who doesn't even want anything to do with him.... He just starts at me with a blank look and said... I have to look after my dogs... I said great, so just send a big bag of dog food every month to the house.

CHAPTER 3

Another horror story

J ames also introduced me to his old friend from the UK who was visiting and his story is even more enlightening.

I only met him for about an hour with James one afternoon while James was staying at out hotel. Anyway, this poor guy was in his mid 70's and was married to a younger Thai woman and sadly, she dropped down dead from a heart attack while they were walking together near their UK home in London. Now it that was not a hard enough blow, listen to the rest of his story....

They also had a house here in Thailand that was all paid for and furnished which they used when staying in Thailand. Because his wife had died, he had to come to Thailand to sort out the house, bank accounts (with over a million Baht (GBP 20K in their Thai bank accounts) and all the paperwork etc. The house should in theory revert to him as there were no children and he was the legal husband.... He cannot legally own the land unless he set up a Thai company.

When he arrived, he found that the house had been broken into (by her relatives and family members) and all the furniture was gone. The bank accounts had been emptied (He had no idea how they managed to do that without the death certificate, but in Thailand – anything is possible). He was then chased out of the village and told to never come back. He was scared to death and had to leave Thailand ASAP.

However, 6 months later, and at 70 odd years of age, he now has a new Thai girlfriend and was visiting her nearby with plans to take her on holiday to Vietnam and more.

CHAPTER 4

German guy living in Chonburri

W e also have a German guy booked in for 3 nights, (I don't know his name as I write this). He keeps himself to himself and is about 46 years of age. His girlfriend looks about 16 years of age in her uniform..... but my wife has informed me she must be about 20 ish as she is studying at the University. This is a fairly common thing we see with older guys and young students that have met on some dating website like "Thai Friendship" on the internet.

These guys are fairly smart in their operations as they already live in Thailand and have a business or online business, nice car and I assume loads of girlfriends chasing them. They use the dating sites to find "nice educated Thai girls" instead of the typical "bar girl" and "hooker type" that most guys seem to end up with. The University girls are FREE (no money needs to be paid to them as they do not want to be seen as hookers) The guy(s) pretend to be looking for a serious wife and give the same old story about wanting to build a house in Thailand... This makes the girls go crazy and they will sleep with you and be your girlfriend even if you have two heads and one leg and in a wheelchair!

So this German guy spends the daytime around the pool on his computer and takes the student to her lessons in the morning...

back again at lunchtime for more shagging as curtains drawn and then back to school for the afternoon session. Evenings they go out for dinner and then back to the room for more shagging till the morning. How do we know they are shagging...? The bin has many used condoms in it every morning.

CHAPTER 5

Old Guy from the UK

T he old boy in a previous story, reminds me of another guy we had a few months ago, so before I forget, let me tell you briefly about this 72 year old guy from England.

He was very overweight, bulging eyes, red face and big belly and not very fit to say the least. He booked into our resort with a really nice girl who worked at a local government office. She must have been late 20's or early 30's. Very attractive with her own car but she was acting like his slave… Going to the shops for him, doing all his little jobs that most of us would do ourselves.

Anyway, after a few days, I found out he was still married and still had a wife of 35 years back in the UK and he had no intention of getting a divorce. He told me he just comes over for a bit of fun! I can only assume that he used the old,

"I'm looking for a wife and want to build a house" story on her.

I felt really sorry for her, as again, every morning there were used condoms in the bathroom bin so he was definitely shagging her every night as well, and he had no intention of marrying this lovely girl.

CHAPTER 6

Rob from USA

Well Rob was a really nice guy, he'd booked a week with us and we had many interesting evening chats in the Cabana near the pool. He was about 60 ish and had a fairly attractive older type girlfriend (probably in her 40's) who still worked doing "massage in Pattaya...!"

I believe they met on the internet and she had told my wife, he had already paid about 500,000 Baht for her to have a boob job and also a tummy tuck. He also sends her money every month and was here at our hotel looking around her village to buy her land and build a house! (About 400,000 for the land and another 1 million for the house)!

He has no intention to take her to the USA or for him to retire to Thailand (not for quite a few years anyway) However, he is still sending her money every month and only intends to come to Thailand once or twice a year... I kid you not... He is besotted with her but to everyone else, we see a very lucky older type bar girl indeed. I sincerely hope they will be happy and stay together for a long long time....

BUT as we all know, and you will soon understand reading my stories about the "Lambs to the Slaughter", most guys end up losing everything because they fall in love with the girl and cannot understand that "she does not love him"... She only loves him as long as he keeps sending money or paying for everything. To the girl it is, (95% of the time) a business decision and he is her winning lottery ticket. You will most likely become the walking bank ATM for the girl and her entire family.

CHAPTER 7

Swiss guy wants a big Thai wedding!

H ere is an interesting story about a Swiss guy, coming to Thailand to marry his Thai girlfriend and then take her back to Switzerland. He wants to have a big Thai wedding but his girlfriend does not... which is pretty rare I would think.

His girlfriend is actually one of the girls that helped Paul, (see the first story about Paul) get away from the nightmare gold digger, the one that was crying because she couldn't get him to understand her.

Anyway, she has told my wife....

That her future husband – a Swiss guy, who has just arrived in Thailand, wants to have a typical Thai style wedding! However, the nice and honest Thai girlfriend, DOES NOT WANT HIM TO DO THAT, because it will incur massive expense. All she wants, is a small, local family do with a simple ceremony and then a register office wedding in Switzerland. She is a not a stupid young gold digger but a very sensible, 43 years old educated lady, separated for 9 years from her previous Thai partner (never married) and has 2 daughters. A very nice lady indeed.

If he does do the full Thai style wedding – He will pay for:

- Several days of celebration for the whole village

- All the food and drink the whole village consumes (and steals) during the said days.

- The cow and pigs that will be slaughtered for the feast

- The dowry (could be £1000 to 10,000) who knows what the family will demand

- Gold for the wife and family (again it will be in the £1000's of pounds)

- The rings – (dependent on how big a face your bride wants to portray)

- Accommodation for all the people coming in from other areas

- Then the honeymoon – If he has any money left.

- Flowers, brides dress, grooms suit, monks, invitations, photographer, souvenirs and much more....

- And don't forget all the ongoing monthly financial commitments that the family WILL EXPECT because YOU have now shown them, how very wealthy "all foreigners" really are!

It's bad enough that virtually ALL Thais believe or are taught from birth, that ALL FOREIGNERS are wealthy.

The Thai's really do not have any concept in their minds that, ALL countries have rich and poor people and let me tell you, in my experience of coming to Thailand for 27 + years... There are a lot more WEALTHY Thai people in Thailand percentage wise, than there are, wealthy people in most other countries.

The issue, here in Thailand, is that Thais cannot or WILL NOT marry anyone below their current status. Therefore a lower level Thai girl (That's virtually all the girls who have not completed university and all the village girls with no education) have, ZERO chance of marrying any Thai guy that has a decent job or income...

WHY? because his family WILL NOT ALLOW IT TO HAPPEN.

Hence they all look to find a "foreigner" to marry.

It really is beyond belief what "some" foreigners will do –

What they fail to understand is, these days, many many people, myself included, DO NOT and WILL NOT play the stupid rip off money games that many (not all), Thai families try to impose on the girls and their new found farang husbands. They use their daughters like a business deal.... mainly to get a large lump some of money in... and when the marriage fails, the family simply TELLS the daughter, to get rid of the CASH COW foreigner, that has stopped producing the past and present money flow and FIND AN-OTHER ONE.

This Swiss guy has found a really nice and honest girl that does not want him to waste £10,000's on a Thai wedding but he is apparently adamant that he wants to do it.

CHAPTER 8

Murdered his wife in Phuket

When I was living and working in Phuket some years ago, I met a German guy that told me his hard luck story about his marriage and his wife.

He was a successful restaurateur in Germany and met his dream girl some 5 years previously. They married and were apparently very happy for about 4 years as he had lots of money and they set up a restaurant in the Kamala beach area of Phuket.

Fast forward 5 years and he was sitting with me outside the Banana disco on the beach road in Phuket, telling me what had happened..

The restaurant eventually failed and over the last 5 years all the money was spent. He thought his wife truly loved him, but her family "TOLD" her to dump him as the money had run out and find a new CASH COW husband. She had apparently left him a few weeks before I met him and she was now living with an American Forex trader in Singapore.

However, as we were sitting there chatting over a beer, a taxi pulled up and the German guy I was chatting with, started staring very intently into the taxi, he then jumped up, ran to the taxi and tried to open the rear door but the taxi sped away!

He comes back to the table all agitated and said,

"That was her in the taxi, she told me she was in Singapore but she is lying again".

I tried to calm him down but he was really depressed and going on about how he had put his whole life and savings into their marriage and her family just convinces her to dump him. He told me, he really loved her and she loved him, but now had nothing left, the business and all the money was gone.

The next day, I met up with him again and he told me, he had tracked her down and he had arranged to have a meeting with her to talk that evening. I wished him luck and hoped it all went well.

I didn't see him again after that day.... but his "picture and crime" was the main news in the Phuket Gazette that week. He was on the run from the police as they had found his wife murdered and disfigured with her private parts cut out!

About a year later there was an article in the Bangkok post –

They had tracked him down in Germany and he was being extradited back to Thailand to face charges on his wife's murder. There are so many cases of foreigners losing EVERYTHING because they believed their Thai wife at the time but nobody knows what the future holds.

Never ever, move all your money or assets to Thailand

Always leave something in your home country – Just in case it does not workout.

CHAPTER 9

Educated Thai girl rips
off Swedish guy

One of my wife's co workers, (at a bank she used to work at), was an educated Thai girl earning approx 40,000 + Baht per month. She was fairly attractive and 42 years of age with a Swedish boyfriend. She had travelled to Sweden a few times (he paid for the tickets) and he had been to visit her in Thailand quite a few times.

He worked for a Swedish airline company and used to get subsidised flights and was madly in love with this girl. He was not rich by any means and did not even own his own house, but he used to send her money (only god knows why, as she was earning a very good income anyway and even owned land and property etc.) He was even going to help her buy some more land as she wanted to build an apartment building on it!

We are talking about millions Baht (1 million Baht = £23,000 approx)

She however, was not in love with him and had admitted to my wife and her other close friends that she was messaging other guys and "he was not rich enough for her" but she didn't want to stop the money flow and the possibility of "him getting a loan in Sweden" to help her buy the land. Even when he came to Thailand, she wouldn't even let him meet her family... and stayed with him in a hotel while he was in Thailand visiting her.

They met on either Facebook or Thai Lovelinks (I cannot remember which one) and luckily for the Swedish guy... he came across a duplicate profile (on same the website) with her picture but under a different name...!

Anyway, he made contact with her via a new profile (he had created with a different name and picture of himself), to see if it was really her and to catch her out. Sure enough, he realised it was her and they had a big argument as he thought she loved him also and they were going to get married and he was sending her money etc.

Luckily for him, he found out she was cheating on him before he got the loan and sent her a very large sum of money. Their relationship ended and although he was devastated for several months, he soon met another girl via Facebook (my wife showed me the posts and pictures of him on Facebook with his new girlfriend.) So hopefully, he is in a better relationship now.

What happened to her? – Here is KARMA in action

The Thai girl from the bank has since, dated several guys and has been milking them all financially and been on several holidays and even, posts on Facebook all about her newest boyfriend of the moment etc.

About 7 months ago, we heard, she was going to marry another guy who also lived in Sweden and he was "apparently", quite rich and surprisingly, she had, left her job in the bank! to move to Sweden and marry this new guy.

My wife told me that, giving up a well paid bank job (that this girl had been in for 20 + years) is a really big deal, as she would also lose a very good pension and there would be no way of getting her job back with the bank if things didn't work out!

She had also, "sold some land she already owned, for several millions of Baht" and the money was supposed to be used between them or whatever, in the marriage. (I don't know those details)

Anyway, she got her Fiancée visa sorted out and was intending to get married in Sweden. On arrival in Sweden, they had a massive row and split up within the first few days because... "She did not have the money from the land anymore." She had told her future husband, she had used the money to pay off some of her debts...

He apparently went nuts and kicked her out. She then spent the next several months living with "his friend" who had felt sorry for her and taken her in because she had no money, nowhere to go and could not even afford to change the airline ticket to get back to Thailand early. She had also not even told her family in Thailand she was getting married.

On her return to Thailand, she couldn't even return home, as she had "LOST FACE" and had to stay in Bangkok with another of her friends and could not come back to her home city where she had "left her bank job" and told her work friends and associates, "she was going to Sweden to marry a rich guy".

Last we heard from her, was a month ago, when she contacted my wife asking her to go into business with her and loan her a million + Baht to do some land or property deal....

Of course my wife declined.

CHAPTER 10

Nice German Guy but his wife has a Gik

Here is an interesting story that concerns a German guy we will call Eric for the sake of anonymity. He has stayed with us several times before and this is what happens every time....

Eric is a perfect guest and a really nice friendly guy. Loves his wife to death and does anything she wants. His Thai wife of 14 years, always flies to Thailand a week before him (They live together in Germany). She books the rooms and then stays the first week with us... with her GIK.

A "GIK" is a Thai boyfriend for a married woman. So she has a week of shagging and then the "GIK" leaves and she goes to pickup her unsuspecting husband Eric, at the airport. They then stay together for 3 weeks and either Eric flies home first and his wife follows a week or so later, or they fly back together.

And Yes.... She comes back here again with the GIK for another week of shagging.

Now, you would think "the wife" would have a bit more of a conscience and use a different hotel to stay with her GIK... But, no, she stays here and openly flaunts around with her boyfriend as if it were all perfectly normal. She even tells my wife that her husband has no idea about him and her husband loves her so much... That he is totally devoted to her...

I kid you not

CHAPTER 11

A very unusual booking

A few months ago we had an online booking come through at 8 PM by email from Agoda but it had a strange request. The booking was for 2 men and a female and they wanted to "pay cash on arrival" and just use the room till 4 AM, when they would then be going back to Bangkok via car.

They also said, they would only be chatting by the pool and had two more people coming at about 10 PM and would pay us an extra 400 baht making 1400 baht. We agreed as it seemed like they only wanted to kill time and have a chat with friends around the pool.

They arrived an hour later at 9 PM. Two older guys and what looked like a bar girl in a short skirt and tattoos... They told us, "Their friends were arriving later", and just sat by the pool smoking and chatting. The girl did get in the pool several times for a swim and to lay on the blow up air beds but everything was normal.

At 10 PM another car arrived with an older woman and what looked like schoolgirl or student about 14 years of age in her school uniform. We assumed it must be the wife and daughter of one of the guys already checked in.

This was all recorded on our on CCTV cameras.

They all went into the bungalow for about 10 minutes and then the bar girl and one of the men, came outside and started chatting and smoking again. She went back in the pool for a while and then just sat there smoking and chatting also. Every 20 minutes or so, the guy outside or the bar girl, went back into the bungalow for a while and sometimes the first guy was smoking outside and the other guy was inside. This went on for several hours and at no time, did we ever see the older woman or the school girl come out.

Apparently, they all left in the two cars at about 4 AM (my wife was still watching the CCTV and her Thai TV program) I was sleeping.

Conclusion

At first we thought it was a simple meeting between friends and the wife and daughter of one of the guys.

BUT that was not the case.....

The bin in the bathroom had several used condoms, the bath towels were all used and it was obvious that the two guys were taking turns and shagging the young girl. The older woman must also have been in on it, as it is fairly common here in the University area for an older women to act as MAMASAN for the students, who want to make extra money letting older guys use them.

A mamasan is like a female pimp who organises the customers for the girls, they also have a mamasan in most bars to keep all the girls in order... She is the big boss for the bar girls.

Apparently the young students can make a lot of money from older Thai men.. From what I can gather, it's a service for Thai men only, the police, government officials, rich Thai businessmen and even school teachers are the customers and it's all arranged through the mamasan.

A strange evening indeed.

CHAPTER 12

Retired Rich Danish guy

Here's a new story, hot off the press. My wife has just told me about a situation that is going on right now.

A rich guy from Denmark married his Thai wife 5 years ago. He was 65 and she was 36 years of age. He has a house in Denmark and has just finished building a big house with swimming pool over here in Thailand. He is retired now at 70 years and living here in Thailand with her 8 year old daughter and her family. She (his wife) wanted to go back to Denmark and continue working as a line manager in a factory. He has offered her 60,000 Baht per month to stop working in Denmark and come and live with him in their new house in Thailand. But she has refused…!

Her Thai family take him to Makro (Like Costco) in their car to buy all his supplies every week and he lives alone and cooks for himself.

He is apparently very rich, but she does not want to live with him in Thailand, she wants to stay in Denmark. The talk is that she must have a GIK (boyfriend) in Denmark.

If he leaves her… He will lose it all as he has built the house in Thailand (all for nothing) as it will all be in her name. The poor guy is retired and 70 years of age and wanted to spend the rest of his life in Thailand with her…. But all she wants to do is enjoy her new life in Denmark…. She doesn't even want to take her 8 year old "Thai" daughter from her previous marriage to Denmark as her family are looking after her in Thailand…. How convenient.

So that's a typical example of a Thai girl marrying an older guy.

==================================

Now, please understand that not all Thai women are like the above, I have been happily married for 10 years and received a lovely comment today from a gentleman that claims he has been happily married to a Thai for nearly 20 years. She was a virgin when they met and he is 69 and she is 59 now with a 15 year old son between them. None of her family ever asked him for money and they have had a really good relationship.

CHAPTER 13

*Divorce rate between Thai girls
and Foreign husbands*

This is an interesting article from The Nation, a national newspaper in Thailand and if these statistics are just from Khon Kaen, I cannot imagine what the Foreigner to Thai girl divorce rate is for the whole country!

Khon Kaen – A total of 142 divorce cases were sent to the Khon Kaen Civil Court in just three months, most of them involving with Thai women seeking divorce from their western husbands, a senior judge said Saturday.

Patikorn Khonpipit, chief justice of the Juvenile and Family Court in Khon Kaen, said the divorce cases reached the court during July 1 to September 30.

He said most of the cases were filed by Thai women who wanted to get divorce from their foreign husbands.

The judge said Khon Kaen was one of the provinces with a lot of Thai women getting married with foreigners and many of them became disillusioned later so they filed for divorce.

Source - The Nation

CHAPTER 14

NEW THAI POLICE MONEY MAKING SCAM

The Thai police have come up with a NEW money making scam. They are stopping all foreigners (farangs) and asking to see their driving licence.

If you don't have an INTERNATIONAL DRIVING LICENCE = 1000 B on the spot fine.

Although up till now, I believed it was perfectly legal to drive on a British or (your own countries) driving licence for up to one year. You can still hire a motorbike or car on a standard British driving licence!

Problem is, it costs about £20 (1000B) to get an International driving licence in your home country before travelling to Thailand. So either way – you have to pay!

This seems to be a big money spinner for them as they can get farangs to pay 1000 B where as most other fines for anything else seem to be between 200 (for Thais) and 400 B for the rest of us.

We see road blocks everyday on the main roads and they normally check cars for No tax disc, and motorbikes for no helmet or driving licence... Although they seem to be cracking down on the motorists....

It's really only about the money as there are still 1000's motor-bikes (and cars)

- Illegal and VERY noisy after-market exhausts Cars and bikes

- Underage – I see kids of 10 riding old motorbikes up and down the road

- Young kids RACING their motorbikes with really loud exhausts at flat out speed – every day – The Noise is unbelievable

- Everyone drives the wrong way (towards you) in the motorbike lane!

- 4 out of 10 motorbikes – do not have a working rear red light at night

- 100's of bikes per day go by me with 3 or more people on the bike

- Everyday I see women carrying a baby in their arm riding a bike

- Many are even texting, or holding a drink while driving the bike.

- Virtually EVERY rear passenger has their head in the phone ALL the time

- Then when they are old enough to stand, they are placed in front of the rider holding on to the motorbike handle bar.

- Then there are all the dogs in the front basket or sitting on the rear seat

- Loads of bikes are not taxed or don't even have number plates as they are only used locally in the villages.

- The other day I saw, this guy balancing a hot "bowl of noodle soup" in one hand and trying to ride with the other!

NONE of these offences or safety issues are ever addressed and the police NEVER chase anyone for ANY of the above crimes...!

It's truly incredible to watch as they are only interested in COL-LECTING MONEY at THE ROAD BLOCKS.

CHAPTER 15

My first Thai wife

This is one of my own stories... A true account of what happened with a Thai girlfriend I had between divorcing my 1st Thai wife Sian and meeting my Filipino wife.

So in 1991, while on holiday in Thailand, I met Sian and over the following year, I had massive issues trying to get her into the UK. Visa's refused, back and forth to Thailand, lived with her in hotels for 3 months in Australia, NZ, Indonesia and Singapore while waiting for Visa appointments. Only to be refused again! It was a living nightmare...

Then I consulted a very expensive immigration lawyer in London, that advised me to get several European holiday Visa's in her passport, as though we were on a European honeymoon, then apply for entry to the UK from a British Embassy in Europe, reason being, they were less likely to refuse her a visa.

We got the European visa's no problem... France, Italy and Germany... but not the UK and I am British! and just paid £40,000 income tax that year! I was fucking livid to say the least. We flew to Italy and went into the British embassy to apply again... He took one look at her passport and saw a tiny rubber stamp in the back. Then called us into an office and told me, He understood what I was trying to do and truly felt sorry for me, as he saw many British guys trying to get their wives or fiancée's into the UK. But whenever they see the little stamp... They had to refuse the Visa and refer us back to Bangkok.

I was going out of my mind, as now we were in Europe but I needed to get back to the UK... I had a business to run and had been away for far too long already. We headed for France where I had to leave Sian in hotel in Nice, South of France, all alone for a week, not being able to speak English or French, I left money and food etc. while I flew back to the UK to deal with some serious business issues.

I did eventually get her into the UK (Cannot put here in print how I did it) and then got a top lawyer in London to fight the appeal but it took over a year and I estimated £36,000 in costs of travel, staying in hotels and legal fees etc. Anyway, there's so much more and that's such a long and story in itself, so I will save it for another time as so many things happened between us over the years.

So fast forward 7 years. My previously successful business finished a year after getting Sian into the UK. Most of my money was used up trying to get various other businesses off the ground and my 3 houses were all repossessed during a property crash. We'd travelled and lived in South Africa, the Philippines, the USA, Australia, New Zealand and also spent many years living in Thailand.

Although I wasn't totally broke, I still had some money saved for a rainy day in an offshore account. So we eventually came back and lived in the UK where I was self employed and working with a networking marketing company and Sian was working part time.

The problem was... I'd become really sick and tired of her drinking, gambling, going out with her friends every weekend and even week nights, to house parties, casinos or nightclubs... and well... like I mentioned before, that's another long story...

Anyway, we had a huge row and separated... I went to Bali, Indonesia to do some recruitment work with the company I was involved with. Sian moved in with her friends, still in the UK. When I came back after 2 months, I contacted her... to more or less see if there was anything left of our relationship... She told me she was having a baby by some guy at her work place. So that was the end of that.

CHAPTER 16

Nightmare girlfriend

I then moved back to Thailand and continued with my recruiting work. I had a nice apartment on the 23rd floor of a high rise and a view to die for... looking out over the Bangkok skyline the view and evening lights were incredible, it was on a par with Hong Kong. Girls were always available, day or night and I had several regular girlfriends but nobody special that I wanted to have move in and live with me.

Until I met Pim...

Pim was a stunning 23 year old, tall Asian angel with a beautiful face and as I truly thought at the time, a nice personality. She had only been working in the Go Go bar for a couple of months when saw her for the first time, she was dancing totally naked in a line up of 20 other naked girls. This was in a 3rd floor top level bar in the Nana Plaza in Bangkok.

I fell in love with her immediately... I paid her bar fine and spent a whole week with her. Even though she was quite tall for a Thai girl about 5 feet 6 inches, she had beautiful small tits and the smallest, tightest pussy I had ever experienced. I eventually paid (another large bar fine, cannot remember how much) for her to leave the bar completely and we lived together for about 18 months.

During that time, I took her to Cape Town, South Africa where we stayed for 3 months, then Malaysia where we lived in Ferrangi beach for a month... Then we ended up in Phuket, Thailand, my most favourite place to live... And I have been all over the world. Yes there are the seedy bar areas like Patong, full of bar girls and lady-boys. But there are also many other nice beach areas like Kata, Kamala and Bang Tao, beautiful high end hotels and resorts, stunning villas and apartments overlooking the ocean. Phuket probably has the best beaches and scenery, I have ever seen anywhere in the world.

Anyway... We'd had a few issues and split up a few times but always got back together... Until this happened.

Nightmare in the police station

While I was on a 2 week trip back to the UK, she had taken my bank book into the bank... I had the ATM card so I assumed, she couldn't withdraw the money. I had placed 40,000 baht (about £1000 pounds) in it, in order to get her a UK holiday Visa... The Visa was refused... that's why I went back to the UK alone.

On my return, I tried to withdraw some cash on my card but it wouldn't work... So I went into the bank, only to be told, my girlfriend had come in with the bank book and emptied the account. It was a joint account and needed two signatures to withdraw money unless using the card, of which, was in my possession. But in Thailand... anything is possible.

She had put a deposit on a new motorbike and even turned up at the airport to meet me with bandages on her face and two black eyes... She'd gone and had a nose job done as well.

I confronted her about the money and she flat out denied taking it... Well... we had a massive row and split up again... This was in Bangkok so I moved back to Phuket to get away from her...

All was good for a few weeks. However, one of her friends had seen me in Phuket and must have told her where I was... So she came to Phuket to find me... It didn't take her long to find me and that's when we met up for a talk... The talk didn't go well as she was accusing me of having another girlfriend (which I did not) because I wouldn't tell her where I was living...

We'd had a few beers and on the way, taking her back to her friends room on my motorbike, where she was staying in Phuket... She started hitting me round the head with a bottle of beer... I stopped the bike and pushed her off... she ended up laying on the roadside... I then drove off but felt bad and turned the bike around... and went back to see if she was OK...

What a mistake that was... She went absolutely nuts, grabbed the key from the bike so I couldn't get away. Then lay into me punching, kicking and biting my arm... I was not responding as that would be very serious in Thailand, but calling out to all these Thai bystanders, for someone to call the police...

They were all just watching and laughing at me (the farang) getting beaten up by his Thai girlfriend who now had a piece of wood, like a fence post and was hitting me with it.

The police eventually turned up... but they wouldn't listen to anything I tried to say... All I got was the hand... as if to say BE QUIET AND WAIT. She was still going crazy, shouting and screaming at me. Eventually, they were all talking away in Thai. Then they, the police and her, started looking for her mobile phone. It was on a neck string... but flew off when she whacked me around the head with it earlier.

Nobody cared or asked if I was OK... I was bleeding with cuts and bruises and a huge burn on my leg from the exhaust. My shirt was hanging off in tatters, it was literally ripped to shreds... it looked like I had been in a bomb blast.

Then guess what...?

I was arrested and taken to the police station as the policeman drove my bike. Now this is when I started to get seriously worried and scared. I had heard so many stories of foreigners being thrown in jail on bullshit charges from their Thai wives or girlfriends, and once they get you in the jail, the extortion starts by the police and lawyers. I'd heard stories of millions of baht having to be paid in bribes to get out of jail.

Anyway, when I was taken into the police station, it was like a scene out of that drug smuggling movie, "Midnight Express" where this evil looking police chief with a peaked cap, big scar on his face was laying back in a chair at his desk, smoking a cigar with his boots up on the desk.

Again, every time I tried to speak, I was given the hand as my girlfriend Pim, rambled on and on in Thai giving them, her version of the event.

I was seriously scared for the first time in my life and was physically trembling in fear, then the police chief said to me in near perfect English,

"You pay for her mobile phone... she say you broke it and now it's gone."

I tried to tell them that she hit me round the head with it and it flew off into the crowd of people, all standing around and watching her attack me. He wasn't interested in the slightest. He just told me I must pay or I stay there till I get someone to bring the money.

Fuck me... my mind was racing, I had to get out of there before she started dreaming up more things they could charge me with like rape... that was a common one and the girl and police could extract 100,000's baht to get away.

So, I said to the big boss policeman,

"OK, if I pay for her phone, can I go home?"

He replied,

"Yes... You go to cashpoint with my man and get 10,000 baht... bring back here".

What... 10,000 Baht! Her phone only cost 4000 baht new... I didn't have a choice and was escorted back to my motorbike where this policeman got on the back and directed me to ride to an ATM cash machine. The first one spat my card out saying "Contact your bank" then luckily the next machine accepted my card and gave me 10,000 baht (about £200 pounds or US$300 at the time)

We then rode back to the police station and I saw Pim smoking a cigarette outside. She followed me in and I handed the money to her in front of the Police chief. She peeled off 5000 and gave it to the big police chief...!

I was free to go as she had her money and the big boss just made 5000 baht as well, for doing fuck all. I didn't care and was so relieved to be free, I jumped on my bike and rode straight home to my apartment.

I was still very scared as she now knew my address I had to write it down in the police station and give a copy of my passport to the police. I knew, she would be causing a lot more trouble and I had just took out a 6 month lease and spent 80,000 baht on furniture, a TV, carpets, bed, wall units and stuff for my new apartment.

My neighbour in the next apartment was a German guy called Uli, who was also a very good friend and had helped me get the apartment a few weeks earlier. He was really shocked when he saw me all battered and bruised and when I told him what had happened.

Well, I told him it wasn't safe for me to stay there any more, especially as my crazy ex girlfriend knew where I lived. I also had my nice new Kawasaki Boss motorbike (60,000 Baht) purchased in "her name" because "farangs" cannot own a motorbike, cars, land or houses on the type of Visa I had at the time.

So I told him to sell whatever furniture he could and I would be in contact by phone and email. I hid the motorbike at another friends house, then left for the airport at first light. I was on the first plane back to Bangkok and then had to wait around another 5 days as I couldn't change my flight back to the UK until then.

Then fuck me... I was walking along the Sukhumvit road and another one of her friends saw me...! I even saw her calling my ex Pim on her phone, while staring at me across the road. I was seriously desperate to get out of Thailand at this point and spent the last 2 days hiding in my hotel room, scared to go out in case she was back in Bangkok looking for me.

Many of the girls knew each other and the bar girl grapevine is a web of connections. You can get virtually anything you want as everyone knows someone who can get drugs, guns, underage girls in fact anything.

The problem was, I was besotted with her and really loved her but several friends had told me she was not what I thought. We'd split up several times but always got back together because of my own stupidity.

However, her stealing the money and what happened in Phuket on the bike and with the police ended the relationship for ever... Even when I was going through immigration and boarding my flight back to the UK, I was still thinking, I could get stopped and arrested as she could have reported me for stealing her motorbike or anything really and she must have guessed I was going to try to leave the country.

On my arrival back in the UK. my elderly mother burst into tears when she saw me as I had bruises and cuts on my face, a huge bite mark with teeth imprints on my arm and a huge burn going septic on my inside calf.

A few weeks passed and I heard that she had turned up at my friends house with a couple of policemen, demanding the motor-bike be handed over to her as it was in her name... But my friend was a very powerful French widow that spoke fluent Thai and was previously married to a very wealthy Thai businessman who had very good connections in the police. So she didn't get the motor-bike, I ended up selling it for 10,000 baht (with no registration papers) to someone through a mate in Bangkok.

I lost my deposit from the apartment I rented in Phuket and never got any money back from furniture that my good German friend Uli tried to sell. That was when I vowed, never to go back to Thailand again.

CHAPTER 17

How I met my Filipino wife

Six months later and I was on my way to Cebu in the Philippines for 3 months... I had been messaging quite a few girls online and decided to go and meet some of them, to see if any were worth pursuing and we clicked. That's where I met Jane, my beautiful Filipino wife that I had a really good 5 years with.

Well, Filipino girls are very different to Thai girls and I had really thought, I had found the girl of my dreams. I'd met 12 girls from the internet dating website and Jane was at the top of the list. 24 yrs old. Still living at home, been to university and never even been in a bar.

Several coincidences happened that I found uncanny. One was on the very first day I had arrived in Cebu, I was crossing the road and two girls were crossing from the other side of the road walking towards me, I smiled at them as they did back to me, I thought one of them was very attractive and then I thought nothing of it...

Until I started meeting with some of my internet dating contacts the next day... The beautiful girl crossing the road was on my list and we had actually been messaging each other but pictures and real life can be very different. I'd met 10 or 12 girls and Jane was at the top of my list, she was also texting me all the time, whereas only a few of the others did and they were not really my kind of girls... I was looking for a long term relationship not a short time fling.

One evening I was standing in a bar and messaging Jane, I was really keen on her so told her to come out that evening for a drink and chat, so we could get to now each other a bit better. But she told me, she couldn't come out alone, especially late at night. But I was thinking.... It wasn't late, it was only 8 PM.

I was a bit pissed off and thought she was making an excuse because she had a boyfriend or something. Then next day she messaged me again, so I told her to come to my hotel. But she had her sister and cousin with her. It was then explained to me that in the Philippines nice girls were not allowed out alone at night. They still had to have a chaperone to make sure they were good girls and protected.

The next few meetings were the same, she was never alone. We had kissed and cuddled in my room but only because her sister was younger and was told to go in the bathroom and wait. Anyway, I needed to get her alone and see if we have any compatibility and got on, so I asked her if she could come away with me for a holiday. She said she wanted to but had to have a good excuse. So she told her parents that she was going to stay at her friends house, a few hours drive from Cebu city...

We took a flight the next day and I rented a beautiful villa on Boracay, a stunning holiday island in the Philippines for 3 months. An American guy owned it and he had several other properties and had lived on Boracay for 20 years. He gave me a great half price deal of US$2000 for 3 months, it was on a hill top and had views over both sides of the island, it even had a private beach in a little protected cove down some long windy steps.

So we were alone at last and getting on really well, we made love day and night and although Jane was not a virgin, she was very inexperienced and willing to learn. I on the other hand was much older at 35 and had loads of experience...

Living on Boracay was heaven, we would walk down to the local market and buy fresh fruit or some seafood to take home and cook. The evenings were the most memorable and spectacular as every evening, all the hotels along the beach, would have tables and chairs on the beach in front of the ocean and sell seafood or whatever. The moonlight would light up the ocean and just walking up and down the beach at night, with the cool breeze, watching the sail boats bobbing up and down was truly paradise on earth.

Then a week in... she told me she had to go back to Cebu as her parents were trying to find out where she was. I was stunned but understood, they must be worried sick. So I bought her a ticket to fly back to Cebu the next day. We had a tearful goodbye and I was wondering what to do next.

She said she was going to sort things out with her parents and then come back, and to wait for her message. But didn't know what to think and couldn't just leave the villa. So out for the next few days I would wander to the market and internet shop in the Post office to check my emails. Walk down the beach at night, fending off all the offers from lovely young girls who used to call out,

"Hello Sir, Can I come home with you Sir."

Even the Philippines has its bars and vampires of the night. So a few days go by and then I received a text from Jane,

"Can I bring my parents to Boracay, they want to meet you?"

I was shocked and also happy so replied immediately,

"Yes of course Jane, when can you come?"

"They're too scared to go on an air plane but there's a big ferry that goes from Cebu to Boracay every evening. We can get that tonight and it arrives in the morning, then we have to get the small boat to Boracay. I think 10 am tomorrow."

"Great, I will give you the money back for the boat fares etc. later. See you tomorrow at about 10 am. Call me when you get on the small boat and I will walk to meet you at the jetty."

I was more than ecstatic, Jane was coming back and with her parents to meet me. She must have told them the truth and now they need to do the right thing and check me out.

Next day, I met them off the boat and we all went for a meal... I took them to a pizza place but they were not impressed and only into Rice and fish and basic Filipino food. We all got on OK and they speak English in the Philippines so communication was not a problem. 3 days later and we were sending them off on the boat for their overnight trip back to Cebu.

Jane stayed with me and we had an amazing 2 more months on Boracay to get to know each other. I knew after the first month, I wanted to marry Jane as that was the only way to get her into the UK on a permanent basis. So we discussed it and she said, yes she wanted to get married and <u>no she did not want to have babies</u>. Because, I told her, I'd had a vasectomy several years before and I already had two children from my first marriage and told her I didn't want to go through that again.

So then came another, I believe, fated coincidence.

My flight was leaving for the UK on Sept 12. Now because of the nightmare situations I had been through in the past with my ex wife and also Pim... both being refused visas several times, no way was I expecting the British embassy in Manila to give Jane a Fiancée Visa easily. Not only is it bloody expensive and involves an in depth interview in Manila, the waiting list time was usually 3 - 6 months for an appointment.

So I was planning on flying home and sorting out Jane's air-plane ticket, after she got her Visa, most likely in 4 or 5 months time. I got all the documents together and printed off the Visa application form and posted them recorded delivery to the British Embassy in Manila.

Two weeks later we get a phone call from Jane's parents... The visa appointment had arrived and is on Sept 11. The day before I fly back to the UK. Now that was uncanny and we were happy but never expected things to work out so well. We could then both fly to Manila and then I put her on a flight back to Cebu and I fly back to the UK. She could follow me later, provided she passed the interview and got the Visa.

On Sept 10th... we left Boracay and checked into a hotel in Manila.

Next day we go to the British embassy only to find it is all cordoned off and more or less closed for the day. The reason was, it was the anniversary of the twin towers Sept 11.

However, they were allowing some people in and Jane was on the list of Visa interview appointments. In she went and I wished her luck, not believing she would get a Visa so easily. I went off to find a coffee shop and expected a 1 - 2 hour wait.

It could only have been 20 minutes later, when Jane was on the phone telling she passed and got the Visa. We just had to wait an hour and then come and pick up her passport and Visa at the embassy.

I was totally stunned... but now the universe pulls another fast one on us.

We picked up her passport and Visa at 12 PM and I was flying out on Qatar airways with a connecting flight in Doha the next day at 11 AM. We got a taxi to the Qatar airways office in Manila and walked in, I told them I was on a flight to London tomorrow the 12th Sept and asked if by any chance there were any available seats on my flight?

They had one seat left on the Doha to London leg and a cancellation had just come in for the Manila to Doha leg!

I remember just staring at the woman who was smiling and asking me if I wanted to book the last seat. My mouth was wide open and Jane asked me what was wrong? I told her nothing wrong, just unbelievable, this is all falling into place like magic.

Jane and I flew back to the UK together the next day. We married in the UK 3 months later and guess what the next available marriage date was at the registry office when we applied?

February 14 Th Valentines day

Now if you don't believe the universe guides us and helps us when we are on the right path, good luck to whatever you believe but for me. Meeting Jane and how it all unfolded with the 1st meeting, dates, flights, appointment and even wedding day. There's a lot more to life than most people realise.

SO WHAT HAPPENED NEXT

Well, we were really happy for at least 4 years but in the 5th year, as she got to age 29 and all her friends were having babies, she, although I had told her at the beginning of our relationship I didn't want any more kids and had had a vasectomy.

And she also told me, she didn't want to have kids either.

She started asking questions about vasectomy reversals and her personality had seriously changed. And after putting ALL the money I had... and another ten grand on credit cards, into building a hillside home for us overlooking the ocean with a pool in Cebu.

She had seriously changed, spending all her spare time on Facebook or out with her Filipino friends. Most weekends, I assumed she was staying over with her friends, she didn't want to go out in the evenings any more, in fact she was like a completely different person.

Then I found out she was not staying at her friends house, she was having an affair with her driving instructor...! And not only that... she was pregnant.

So that was the end of my relationship with Jane.

We split up as I told she needed to move in with him. They were not happy, argued constantly and she admitted to me later, she made a big mistake and still loved me but I was not prepared to take her back with his child. He was so possessive and would never have left us alone. I was devastated and incredibly upset, I think it took me over a year to get over that relationship.

I eventually sold the house in Cebu, it took 4 years and we split the proceeds but that's another nightmare story as the developer died and we ended up with a half finished house, then we found he didn't even have planning permission, so nobody wanted a half finished house with no papers.

Jane and I would have serious arguments and screaming matches down the phone. She had even moved house with him and wouldn't tell me her address. I was £10,000's in debt on my credit cards and had no back up savings. Everything went into finishing off the house and clearing the stage payments to the developer.

Jane was not helping at all and I think, she was hoping, I would eventually give up and she would get to keep the house in Cebu. However, I had found a really good, tenacious and honest real estate agent, I found out much later he was disabled and came from Hong Kong but married to a Filipino. All the other agents dropped me like a hot stone when they found out about the planning permission, but he didn't. Every few months he would do another viewing and I would do do internet marketing to help get people looking at the house, as EVERYTHING I had went into that house.

Four years later, we got an offer, from a rich Filipino guy, who was watching the build and also owned several other houses on the development. The house would have been worth £200,000 with the planning permission and we were trying to sell it for £120k. He offered £80K... He also had contacts in the planning office and said he could get the paperwork sorted... it was all basically down to bribes.

After another huge argument with Jane on the phone, telling her the house would get either repossessed or knocked down, because the government had already started sending tax demands and inquiring about the paperwork. She agreed to sell. We both flew to Cebu and signed the deed of sale and we both ended up with £40k each. She bought another house in Cebu and I was out of debt at last.

So that's the story of what happened to Jane and I can assure you, every word of this story is true.

As for myself now, I'm semi retired and very happily married for the last 10 years to a really nice, educated and honest Thai lady. We've built a hotel and pool resort in Thailand and have been amazingly happy for 14 years and counting.

I hope you found these stories entertaining and enlightening,

Comments and positive reviews are much appreciated and help my books in the Amazon Algorithms.

Best regards,

Dave James

Check out my other books;

Lambs to the Slaughter 2: Love, Scams and True stories of Thai girls.

Escape from Tyranny: True Earth and the search for more land beyond the Antarctic ice ring.

Everyone is Asleep: But a few have woken up and live lives of total amazement.

Astrology of Transgender's Relationships and Compatibility: Synastry, Transits and Reincarnation.

Freedom in Thailand: How we escaped and built a bungalow and pool resort.

Authors email address: dave-james@gmx.com

Printed in Great Britain
by Amazon

28463606R00036